PYTHON PROGRAMMING FOR ADVANCED

The Updated Advanced Guide to Master Python Programming Step by Step In A Few Days with Machine Learning and Data Science Resources

(Vol. 3)

AUTHOR

BILL STEVEN

This document is geared towards providing exact and reliable information with regards to the topic and issue covered. The publication is sold with the idea that the publisher is not required to render accounting, officially permitted, or otherwise, qualified services. If advice is necessary, legal or professional, a practiced individual in the profession should be ordered.

- From a Declaration of Principles which was accepted and approved equally by a Committee of the American Bar Association and a Committee of Publishers and Associations.

Table of Contents

Introduction

The Python language is often considered one of the best coding languages out there for helping you to see some amazing results with any project that you would like to undertake. Sometimes, when we first get started with our research into coding languages, we are going to feel a bit overwhelmed by all of the information that is available for us. We worry that we won't be able to pick out the right one from all of the choices, and we may get frustrated along the way as well.

However, even though there are a ton of programming languages to choose from, and all of them have their own benefits to look into, one of the best general-purpose coding languages that you can work with for almost any project, whether it is simple or more complex, is the Python coding language.

The Benefits of Python

Even when it is compared to some of the other coding languages out there, Python is going to provide us with a lot of benefits that will make our coding stronger. It is one of the best coding languages out there, for beginners and those who have been doing this coding for a long time. And it won't take long for you to be amazed at all of the work that you are able to do with this language even though it is relatively easy to learn.

The first benefit that you will notice with the Python language is that it is easy to learn. This language was developed with the beginner in mind, in the hopes of bringing more people into coding. Some of the traditional languages were hard and bulky, and unless you were really passionate about some of the work that you were doing with coding, you would probably decide to give up long before anything was done. But with the Python language, things are a bit different. This language as designed to be easy to learn and easy to read, which helped make it possible for more people to get into the world of coding.

Even though you will be pleasantly surprised by how easy it is to learn about the Python language, you will also find that it is a powerful language. Don't let the simplicity of this language fool you; it has enough power to get the work done, no matter how complex or hard the problem is. Even though Python is able to handle some of the basic coding needs that you have, it also has the power to help you to do things like machine learning and data analysis. And if you have spent any time working with these topics, and these ideas, you know that they are not easy.

With this in mind, Python is also going to have a lot of extensions and libraries that help it to work better. This is primarily how you will be able to get Python to work with some of those more complex tasks. You can add these simply by installing them to your computer or system, and the Python language is ready to go when you are. You can then handle algorithms, finish your data analysis, and so much more. There are many Python data science libraries available based on which step of the process you are working on at the time

The large community that comes with Python can be beneficial as well. We will spend some time talking about the various algorithms and more that you are able to do with the Python language and how you can use it along with machine learning. But there are times when you may need to do something different, and you will be confused about how to get this done.

The community that is available from Python will have a ton of programmers, both those who have been coding for a long time, and those who are new to the idea. This is good news for you. The coders who have been in the industry for some time can offer advice and even give you codes that can help you out with any of the coding problems that you run into when working with Python. This can make it a lot easier to handle some of the challenges that are going to come up as a programmer.

And finally, the Python language Is considered an object-oriented programming language, or OOP. This may not make a lot of sense now, but it is going to be so important when you get started with your own coding in Python. It basically separates out everything into classes as well as objects that are able to go into those classes, which will ensure that all of your information is located right where you would like to find it.

As you can see, there are a number of benefits that come with working on the Python language. You will quickly see that Python is able to handle all of the major tasks that you would like with data analysis and machine learning. Don't let some of the simplicity and ease of use confuse you; Python has all of the power and the features that you need to get the work done.

Ways That We Can Use Python

There are so many different ways that we are able to use the Python language for our own needs. You will find that this is one of the best coding languages out there to help out with a lot of the different projects that you are trying to focus your time and attention on. Whether you are creating an app that you would like to sell, trying to make things easier for some of your own programming needs, or you want to do some coding and some data analysis with this process, you will find that the Python language is one of the best ones to choose.

Even though there are a lot of other coding languages out there that you can use, none of them will be able to compare to the speed, the strength, and the ease of learning and use, as you will find with the Python language. This is part of what makes this language so special.

You are able to work with Python on every project, and even if it is more complex or harder to work on, you will find that it still works for your needs.

There are a lot of different projects that you are able to work on in order to rely on the Python language. And the one you choose is going to vary based on what your goals are. Python works with things like data science, artificial intelligence, and machine learning very well, and you will find that any of the projects that you would like to handle of this sort will kind of just fall in with the Python language as well. Some of the different ways that you are able to work with the Python language in order to get your own coding done includes:

Data science and analysis: Python is great for handling all of the libraries and parts that you need for each and every step in the data analysis process. From gathering the data to sorting through it and cleaning it up, to actually finishing the analysis and creating your own visualizations to see the relationships in the data, you will find that the Python language is going to be one of the best.

Machine learning: Python is also great for machine learning. Since machine learning is able to come in and really help you to figure out some of the algorithms that you need to do. Machine learning is one of the primary ways to handle your data and to help you to complete the analysis that you need. Being able to use the Python language can make this part of the process easier.

Gaming: Gaming is a big industry that is able to rely on Python. You can find a lot of great codes and more that will work in Python and will give some of the games you are creating more power overall. This can make it easier for you to create something brand new.

Creating a website: Even if your business is just looking for a simple way to create a great and interactive website, this is possible with the Python language as well. Python has all of the power and the capabilities that you need in order to handle a lot of the different parts of a website and can make the experience of getting the website done much easier.

Basic coding: While Python is able to handle some of the more complex aspects that come with coding, we will also see that it has some of the power that we need to handle just basic coding as well.

Even though some programmers worry that this language is too simple and easy to use in order to be worth anything for them, this is selling the Python language short.

Chapter 1:   Getting Started with Python

We will be discussing the primary method of getting started with Python.

To start with, you would have to download the appropriate version of Python for your software. Python is valid on a wide range of platforms, so it shouldn't be difficult finding one that matches your system. You can get the Python interpreter for free on the Python main website. Ensure to download a version that is suitable for your operating system to avoid complications when installing the program. The latest version of Python available is the 3.x series. For Linux and Mac OS X systems, Python comes as an already pre-installed package. So, it would not be necessary to install any other software related to Python. However, you might want to get a code editor for writing your codes. The pre-installed versions of Python in some Mac OS X and Linux systems are usually the 2.x series of Python. One significant difference between both series is the change made to the print () statement. So, feel free to upgrade to the 3.x series in your Linux or Mac OS X systems by downloading some files via the official Python website.

Once you have successfully downloaded the appropriate version for your system, the next stage is to install the program. The installation process allows you to make some customization depending on what you want, but it is best to keep it simple and just use the default settings.

Python can be integrated into the command prompt of your system by initializing the final option in a list of the modules available to you.

The next stage is to get and Install a code editor. Although it is possible to code in Python with apps like TextEdit or Notepad, it is usually a much easier task to write your codes with the help of a particular code editor. You would find there are lots of code editors both free and paid from which you can choose from. For example, for the Windows operating system, you can get the Notepad++, for the Mac operating system, you can use TextWrangler, and for other operating systems you can use JEdit.

Once you have completed your downloading bad installing, proceed to the next phase in which you test everything is you installed. Visit the command prompt if you use a Windows system, or Terminal if your system runs on Linux or Mac OS. Enter Python into the command line and click to enter. The Python program would boot up, displaying the version number of the installed program. From there, you would be shown the command prompt of the Python interpreter, which displays as three brackets (>>>). Enter the following line of code shown below and click to enter:

```
print ('Hello, World!')
```

The code should output the result shown as follows, just beneath the command line:

Hello, world!

Basic Knowledge of How Python Works

Keep in mind that Python needs nor be compiled to be executed. Being an object-oriented language in its own right codes in Python can be executed as quickly as they have been modified without having to use a compiler. The fact that it doesn't need a compiler makes it all the more comfortable and quicker to iterate, revise and troubleshoot than most other programming languages of like status.

Also, owing to a high preference for simplicity and readability, you can begin right away to begin coding some simple programs which you can set up in a few moments.

Feel free to try out what you have learned in the interpreter environment. With the interpreter, you can try out your codes, which would not necessarily be added to your program. You can use this environment to groom your coding skills and experiment on specific programs you don't want to include in your programming.

Understand how variables and objects are handled in Python. As an object-oriented language, Python considers everything within it as objects. Another thing to note is that the declaration of variables when starting a program is unnecessary because it can be done at any point in the program without any need to specify what type of variable it is, be it a string, integer, or what have you.

Another thing you can familiarize yourself with is the syntax used by Python. It would help attune you with the method Python uses in handling strings and numbers. To begin, enter the enter interpreter environment. Click to open the Terminal or Command Prompt, depending on your operating system. Input "python" into the prompt as a code and click to enter. You would be directed to the command prompt (>>>) in Python.

If, by now, you haven't already integrated Python into the command prompt of your system, you would have to visit the Python directory to be able to execute the interpreter.

Put your knowledge of Python operators to use in performing simple arithmetic calculations efficiently. Below is a line of code on how to use operators to execute fundamental mathematical problems. Keep in mind that # is used to indicate comments when coding in Python, and the interpreter doesn't execute them with the rest of the codes.

>>> 5 + 6

11

>>> 150 - 5*6

120

>>> (150 - 5*6) / 5 # Division would always output a floating-point (otherwise known as a decimal) number

24.0

>>> (150 - 5*6) // 5 # Floor division (double forward slashes) would remove any decimal in the results

24

>>> 23 % 4 # It calculates the remainder of the division

3

>>> 15.23 * 4.26 / 2.3

28.2086087

You can also attempt to calculate in powers using the double-asterisk (**). It is an operator that indicates powers. As such, Python can make large calculations on numbers. See the sample below:

>>> 8 ** 2 # 8 squared

64

>>> 2 ** 10 # 2 to the power of 10

1024

You can also design and manage variables of your own. For example, in performing algebraic calculations, you can create and assign variables to carry out your calculations. In Python, we assign variables using the sign of equation (=). See the sample below for clarity:

>>> x = 3

>>> y = 9

>>> x * y

27

>>> 27 * x // y

9

>>> x ** 2

9

>>> length = 12 # Any string can be used as variables

>>> breadth = 4

>>> length * breadth

60

You can also practice basic flow control statements and see how good you are at it. Flow control statements let a user take charge of the actions of the program based on certain given conditions. These statements serve as the core of programming in Python and let users design programs which perform many functions depending on the conditions set, and the input is given. For instance, the while statement can be used in calculating a Fibonacci sequence measuring up to 100. Let's consider the sample below:

 # Every number in the Fibonacci sequence represents

 # a sum of two prior numbers

x, y = 1, 2

while y < 100:

print(y, end=' ')

x, y = y, x+y

Here, the sequence can be executed provided (while) y < (is less than) 100.

The result that would be outputted would typically follow after this fashion:

1 1 2 3 5 8 13 21 34 55 89

Rather than separate each value into multiple lines, the end= "command would output all the results on the same line. There are some elements worth noting in this sample, which is critical to the creation of complex Python programs:

Take note of indentation when coding. A colon (:) is an indication that a set of lines are being indented and form a part of the entire block. In the sample above, the lines:

Print(y) and x, y = y, x+y; act as a part of the while block in the code. Thus, adequate programming is a necessity if a program must work.

Also, it is possible to define several variables on one line. Consider the sample above where x and y were both defined on the same line.

When inputting the program into the interpreter directly, take note to include a blank line that ensures that the interpreter is aware of when the program terminates.

Chapter 2: The Importance of Machine Learning

The next thing that we need to take a look at here is why machine learning is seen as such an important thing today.

Things like the growing amount and types of data, the idea that we are able to process things faster and for less money, and that it is easier to store our data until we need it to have all come into play when it is time to work with machine learning.

All of these different things mean that it is very much possible for us to quickly and then automatically produce some of the models that we need. Today, and in the future, we will find that these models are able to handle and analyse ever-growing and more complex types of data while providing us with results that are very accurate and can be presented and delivered faster than ever. And the best part is that this can be done to scale, allowing us the ability to do all o this with however much data we would like.

In addition, we will find that when we are able to take the

time to build up precise models, the organization is going to have a better chance of finding opportunities that are more profitable and will put their business ahead in no time. it is even a great method to use when it is time to avoid some of the unknown risks that could face the business in the future.

Do I Really Need Machine Learning?

It may seem like something out of a book or a movie. Is it really possible to use some coding, even the basic Python code, in order to create algorithms and models that can learn? Is it actually possible for us to take our data and figure out the insights that are in it just by presenting it to a machine learning algorithm?

It may sound like something that is not reality and something from a Sci-Fi movie, but this is definitely the way that the world is taking us right now. By this, we are talking about the wide variety of entities and companies who are already jumping on board with machine learning and using it for some of their needs.

When you spend some time with machine learning, it is not going to take long before you start to see that any industry and any company, who spends time working with data and collecting it will be able to find some kind of value when they work with machine learning as well. And if you plan to do anything with data analysis, and sort through your data to figure out the best course of action to take on a regular basis, then machine learning is definitely something that you need to spend your time with overall.

With this said, there are a lot of companies in many different industries who are relying on machine learning to help them get ahead. Some of the different industries and companies who are already working with this kind of machine learning to help them out with their data analysis will include:

Financial services: There are so many companies within the financial sector who will be able to benefit from using machine learning to help them reach their goals. They will find that machine learning is able to help them figure out who to loan money to, how much to loan out in credit cards, who is the most likely to pay back, and how to avoid things like money laundering and fraud.

Healthcare: This is another industry where we are going to see a lot of big changes when it comes to how they are able to use machine learning. This is an industry that is fast paced, with very little room for error, but it is likely to see a gap in the number of people they are able to employ over the next few years. Some of the models and algorithms that we are able to create with machine learning can help to solve a few of these problems as well.

Oil and gas: There are also a lot of ways that this kind of industry will be able to benefit when it is time to work with machine learning. Some o these are going to include streamlining some of the distribution that the company is using in order to ensure that the process is more efficient and doesn't cost as much, learning how to predict when the sensors of the refinery are going to break, analysing some of the minerals that are found in the ground, and finding new sources of energy to work with. The number of machine learning use cases for this kind of industry is vast and is likely to grow in the future so it is definitely something that these professionals should take a look at.

Government: Government agencies, including those who are in charge of utilities and other parts of public safety, may be able to find machine learning as a useful tool. They are able to take in data to figure out how to keep others as safe as possible in the long run, and it can even come into play when it is time to help the government detect fraud and minimize the amount of identity theft that is happening.

Retail: This is one of those industries where it may seem like machine learning is not going to matter, but when we stop and think about all of the information and data that these companies are able to gather and store about their customers, it is no wonder that they want to get in on some of the work with data analysis and machine learning as well. These retail stores are able to use this information to help them market to their customers better, provide a better recommendation system, pick out which products to sell, and more.

Transportation: And finally, we need to take some time to look at how the transportation industry is going to be able to use machine learning. A good way to look at this is that this industry is going to analyse data to help identify some of the trends and patterns that are found inside. This is able to help us make our routes more efficient and can be good for predicting the potential problems to increase the amount of efficiency that is found in the company.

As we can see, there are already a lot of industries and companies who have seen the value that machine learning is able to provide, and who have decided to jump on board and see how this is able to benefit them as well. Whether you are still considering adding some machine learning to your big data and seeing what insights are in that data or not, you can definitely benefit when it comes to implementing some machine learning in as well.

Machine Learning Methods

While we are here, we need to take a bit of time to look at some of the different types of machine learning algorithms. Each of these is going to be important because they are able to handle a different type of problem that we would like to handle in our algorithms and with our data. We are going to be able to bring up each one based on what we are trying to do with the data at hand.

Machine Learning with Python

Any time that we are ready to handle data analysis, it is important that we take some time to explore the basics of machine learning. It is impossible to conduct a good data analysis without talking about and using machine learning. Machine learning is able to handle some of the different tasks that are needed to take all of that data we have collected and actually create some good insights and predictions out of the hidden patterns that are inside. We will also need to use machine learning, along with the help of codes that are written out in Python, to help us get started with some of our models and algorithms. These algorithms can be trained to take some or all of the data that we have available and sort through it automatically for us. This is how your business is able to go through and get those hidden insights and patterns out of the data, without having to do it manually. With this in mind, we need to take a look at some of the basics that come with machine learning. This will help us to see what machine learning is really all about, how it works, and how we are going to come to rely on it when we handle our own data analysis. The first thing that we need to take some time to explore though is the basics of machine learning.

Machine learning is just going to be a method of data analysis that is able to automate some of the analytical model building that we need to deal with. It is going to be one of the branches that come with artificial intelligence and it will be based on the idea that a system is able to take data and learn from it. This system is also able to use that data to help it identify problems and make decisions. And all of this can be done with little to no intervention from humans. Because of some of the new technologies in computing that are out there, the machine learning that we are likely to see today is not going to be the same as the machine learning that may have been used in the past. Instead, it is born from pattern recognition, along with a theory that says how a computer is able to learn anything that we want, without needing to be performed to that specific task in the first place.

In the beginning, researchers who were interested in some of the different parts of artificial intelligence wanted to get started by seeing if a computer or another system was able to learn from the data that we tried to present to it. The neat thing here is that machine learning is going to have an iterative aspect that will help it to learn. This is important because as the models are exposed to more and more data over time, they will be able to make the necessary adaptations along the way.

What happens with machine learning is that the model is trained to adapt and to learn as needed along the way.

Chapter 3:   Types of Learning Machine

Computers have become an integral part of modern-day operations in almost every sphere of life. Teaching computers how to operate and progressively improve on functionality takes different approaches. The types of machine learning are categorized into taxonomies depending on the underlying problems or the anticipated outcomes. These types of machine learning allow the computer to learn patterns and regularities that are useful across a variety of business and health related fields in the modern world. The following are some of the types of learning algorithms useful in the process of machine learning.

Supervised Learning

Supervised learning occurs where the algorithms create a function that maps raw data into desired outputs. Supervised learning is one of the most common paradigms for machine learning. It is easy to comprehend. The process of implementation of supervised learning may be achieved through systems from the training dataset. The training data or examples contain more than one input and the desired output. The output is also known as a regulatory signal, which is represented within the mathematical model. An array of vectors represents the training example. When provided with data in the form of illustrations, the algorithms may be useful in the prediction of each name. Forecasting takes place in the process of giving a response on whether the answers were right or wrong. The approach allows the algorithms a chance to learn to make approximations over time that allow for the distinction between the labels and the examples. The method makes supervised learning a common option in the process of finding solutions. .

The most common supervised learning approaches include classification and regression. In the case of classification, the use of supervised learning occurs where the outputs may have restrictions to a fixed number of values. Classification typically deals with the identification in a given data set with a view to linking new observations into such categories. On the other hand, the use of regression occurs when the outputs have a wide range of numerical values within a given subset. The goal in both examples is to ensure that machine learning utilizes a fixed set of training examples to make the necessary comparisons on how similar or different a collection of data may be in a given subset. The optimal scenarios in such data sets ensure that the algorithms can determine the class labels for all the unseen occurrences within such a subgroup.

Unsupervised Learning

Machines learning may occur through unsupervised cluster analysis. The approach involves using a set of data that is made up of inputs, which is necessary in the development of a structure. The clustering of data points is an example of unsupervised learning. Unlike in the case of supervised learning, the test data in unsupervised learning does not have labels and is not within a specific classification. Unsupervised learning does not respond to feedback but instead focuses on the commonalities. The method seeks to identify the possibility of commonalities in a given set of data and use these commonalities to develop a pattern. Essentially, this means that the goal is to task a computer with learning how to do something without providing a logical approach to achieve this task. The unsupervised approach is, therefore, more complicated and more complex than the supervised process. This method means using a reward approach to affirm success in the achievement of the tasks without necessarily providing explicit instructions on how to achieve the set goals.

The purpose of the unsupervised approach is more aligned towards the decision-making process as opposed to the mere classification of these data. Unsupervised learning trains the agent to act or respond to tasks based on the reward system or punishment built over time. A computer gradually learns how to navigate past commands without having prior information on the anticipated outcomes. This approach may be time-consuming and tedious. But unsupervised learning can be powerful because it operates from the point of trial and error, which may produce discoveries. Unsupervised learning does not consider any pre-classified information and therefore works from an aspect of the invention.

The unsupervised learning approach is critical in a world where most of the data sets in the world are unlabeled. This undisputable reality means that having intelligent algorithms that can utilize terabytes of unlabeled data and make sense of such information is critical. In the future, there will be different instances where unsupervised learning will become a crucial area of focus. Recommender systems will be a vital area where unsupervised learning will be applicable in the future. The recommender system allows for a distinct link to relationships, which makes it easy to categorize and suggest content based on shared likes.

Reinforcement Learning

Reinforcement learning is useful when the exact models are unrealistic because they rarely assume knowledge of an accurate mathematical model. The approach focuses on how machines should operate to maximize some aspect of cumulative reward. In modern research, the application of reinforcement learning is observed from a behavioural psychology point of view. The method thus functions through interacting with the immediate environment. As we noted earlier, supervised learning operates based on existing examples. The user of interaction with the situation in the case of reinforcement learning indicates a difference between the two approaches.

The application of reinforcement learning in the field of Artificial Intelligence is an indication of the ability of the machines to learn and adjust to new tasks through interactions with the immediate environment. The algorithms adapt to taking specific action based on the observation of the contextual setting. The pattern of behavioural reaction to environmental stimuli is an indication of the process of learning that has become synonymous with artificial intelligence. Every action in reinforcement learning has a direct implication of the operational context, and this reaction provides an opportunity for the machine to receive feedback, which is critical in the process of learning. Reinforcement learning tends to rely on time-dependent sequences or labels. The results in the case of reinforcement learning depend on the connection between the agent and the environmental context. The agent is then given a set of tasks that have a direct implication on the environment. The method then approves a specific reinforcement signal, which provides negative or positive feedback depending on the job and the anticipated result.

Semi-supervised Machine Learning

The use of semi-supervised learning algorithms is essential where there is a small amount of labelled data and enormous amounts of unlabelled data. The method utilizes the combination of both labelled and unlabelled data. The programmer, therefore, uses both data types to identify patterns. The deduced models become the basis on which relationships target variables, and the data examples become easy to identify and analyse. The approach refers to semi-supervised learning because it utilizes data from labelled and unlabelled examples and still makes sense out of this information. Semi-supervised learning is therefore a hybridization of supervised and unsupervised learning approaches. Semi-structured data is used in this case because it does not obey the formal structuring of data models. The tags and other indicators used in the semi-supervised approach aids in the separation of semantic elements. This is essential when there lack enough examples to develop an accurate model. Semi-structured models often make critical sense when there is a lack of adequate resources and limited capacity to increase the available data examples.

The approach allows for the labelling process of the defined data, then it uses the trained model to classify the other data based on the specific model. In some instances, you may find situations where you have a wide range of data with a known outcome, yet also have another set of data that is unidentified. The use of semi-supervised machine learning allows the process to utilize the known data models to build a sequence that can be effective in the course of making labels for the rest of the data sets. As a result, when compared to other models, this approach provides the best option because it is time-saving and also reduces drastically the overall resources used towards achieving the intended outcome.

The creation of an appropriate function when using semi-supervised approaches may be a critical solution in a modern setting where unlabelled data is likely to supersede labelled data in the process of classification. The use of semi-supervised methods in spam identification and detection from standard messages is the most realistic example in the modern world. The use of human knowledge to sieve through such messages would otherwise be impossible to achieve. Using semi-supervised techniques helps in resolving the high dimensionality concern that often affects the process of classification.

One of the most common methods in semi-supervised learning is the use of self-training approaches. The technique allows the class to undergo through a process of learning using a small labelled data set at the initial stages. The classifier obtained from the research is then used to classify a wide range of unlabelled data. Nonetheless, there is still a significant concern associated with the need to address the issue of deciding on highly consistent predictions. The second technique useful in the semi-supervised processes is the generative models. The model operates based on a repetitive approach where unlabelled samples are the heart of the process. The technique demonstrates a higher acceptable performance in the case of the models from this information as opposed to models that are a result of trained examples. Repetitive techniques conventional in the generative method include the interactive training approach.

Chapter 4:   Data Analysis with Machine Learning

Data evaluation is described as a procedure for cleaning, altering, and modelling information to find helpful information for company decision-making. The objective of data evaluation will be to extract useful information out of data and accepting the choice depending upon the information analysis.

Whenever we choose any choice in our daily life is by considering exactly what happened last time or what's going to occur by selecting that specific choice. This is only assessing our future or past and making conclusions in it. For that we collect memories of the past or fantasies of the future. So that's nothing but information evaluation. The exact same matter analyst does for company functions, is known as data evaluation.

Why Data Evaluation?

To increase your company even to increase on your own life, sometimes all you want to do is evaluation!

If your company isn't growing, then you've got to return and admit your errors and make a strategy again without repeating those errors. And if your organization is increasing, then you need to appear ahead to creating the company to grow longer. All you have to do is examine your business data and business procedures.

Data analysis tools

Data evaluation programs make it easier for consumers to process and control information, assess the connections and correlations between data collections, and in addition, it can help to identify patterns and tendencies such as interpretation. Here's a whole collection of resources.

Kinds of information analysis: approaches and methods

There are lots of kinds of data analysis methods that exist according to company and technology. The significant kinds of data evaluation include:

Text evaluation

can also be known as data mining. It's a procedure to find a pattern in massive data collections utilizing databases or data exploration gear. It was used to convert raw information into business details. Business intelligence applications are found on the marketplace that is utilised to take tactical business choices. Overall it provides a means to extract and analyse information and deriving routines and ultimately interpretation of their information.

Statistical analysis

Statistical analysis reveals "what happen?" by using previous information in the kind of dashboards. Statistical analysis contains set, evaluation, interpretation, demonstration, and modelling of information. It analyses a group of information or a sample of information. There are two classes of the kind of evaluation - descriptive evaluation and inferential analysis.

Descriptive analysis

Analyses complete information or even a sample of outlined numerical data. It reveals mean and deviation for constant data whereas frequency and percentage for info data.

Inferential analysis

Investigations sample from comprehensive data. Inside this kind of analysis, it is possible to discover unique conclusions from the very same information by choosing different samples.

Diagnostic analysis

Diagnostic analysis reveals "why did it occur?" by discovering the origin in the penetration located in statistical analysis. This evaluation is beneficial to spot behavior patterns of information. When a new issue arrives on your organization process, then you're able to start looking in to this investigation to locate similar patterns of the issue. Plus, it might have opportunities to utilize similar prescriptions to your new issues.

Predictive analysis

Predictive analysis reveals "what's very likely to occur" using previous information. The easiest example is similar to if past year i purchased two dresses based in my savings and when this season my wages is growing twice then i can purchase four dresses. However, of course it is not simple like this since you need to consider other conditions like odds of costs of clothing has been raised this season or perhaps rather than dresses that you wish to obtain a new bicycle, or you have to get a home!

So, this evaluation makes predictions regarding potential effects based on present or previous data. Forecasting is merely an estimate. Its precision is dependent on how much comprehensive information you've got and how much you really dig inside.

Prescriptive analysis

Prescriptive analysis combines the penetration from all previous analysis to find out which actions to take at a present problem or conclusion. Most data-driven businesses are using prescriptive evaluation because descriptive and predictive analysis aren't sufficient to improve data functionality. According to present circumstances and issues, they examine the information and make conclusions.

Data analysis procedure

Data analysis procedure is nothing but collecting info by employing good tool or application which lets you learn more about the information and find a pattern within it. According to this, you may take conclusions, or you'll be able to acquire ultimate decisions.

Data evaluation consists of the following stages:

- **Data requirement gathering**

First of all, you need to consider why do you want to perform that data analysis? All you have to learn the purpose or goal of accomplishing the diagnosis. You need to select which kind of information analysis you wished to perform! Within this stage, you need to make a decision as to what to examine and how to quantify it, you need to comprehend why you're exploring and what steps you need to use to perform this evaluation.

- Data collection

After requirement collecting, you'll get a clear thought about what you need to quantify and what ought to be your own findings. Now it is time to gather your information based on prerequisites. As soon as you gather your information, do not forget that the accumulated data have to be processed or arranged for evaluation. As you accumulated information from several resources, you should have to maintain a log using a set date and origin of the information.

- Data clean-up

Today whatever information is gathered might not be helpful or irrelevant to your own aim of investigation, therefore it ought to be cleaned. The information that is gathered may include duplicate documents, white distances or mistakes. The information must be washed and mistake free. This stage has to be done prior to analysis because according to data clean-up, your output analysis will be nearer to your anticipated result.

- **Data analysis**

After the information is gathered, cleaned, processed, it's prepared for analysis. As you control information, you might find you've got the precise information you require, or you could have to accumulate more information. In this period, you may use data analysis tools and applications that can allow you to comprehend, interpret, and derive conclusions depending on the requirements.

- **Data interpretation**

After assessing your information, it is now time to translate your results. You're able to pick the best way to express or convey your own information analysis either you'll be able to use only in phrases or possibly a table or graph. Then apply the outcomes of your data evaluation procedure to determine your very best strategy.

Data visualization

Data visualization is quite common in daily to day lifetime; they frequently show up in the kind of graphs and charts. To put it differently, data displayed graphically so it will be simpler for your brain to comprehend and procedure. Data visualization frequently utilized to find unfamiliar facts and tendencies. By detecting connections and assessing datasets, it is possible to get a means to learn meaningful info.

Data evaluation - procedure

Procedure 1.   Data requirements specification

The information required for evaluation relies on a query or an experimentation. Dependent on the needs of these directing the investigation, the information required as inputs into the investigation is closely identified (e.g., population of individuals). Particular factors regarding a people (e.g., age and income) could be defined and got. Information might be either numerical or categorical.

Procedure 2.   Data collection

Information collection is the process of collecting info on targeted factors identified as information demands. The emphasis will be on ensuring honest and accurate selection of information. Information collection ensures data gathered is true like the associated choices are legitimate. Information collection supplies a baseline to quantify along with a goal to improve.

Data is gathered from various sources that range from organizational databases into the info in webpages. The information so obtained, might not be ordered and might contain irrelevant info. Therefore, the accumulated data is needed to be exposed to data processing and data cleaning.

Procedure 3.   Data processing

The information that is gathered has to be processed or organized for investigation. Including structuring the information as needed for the appropriate diagnosis tools. By way of instance, the information may need to be set into columns and rows in a table in a spreadsheet or statistical program. A data model may need to be generated.

Procedure 4.   Data clean-up

The organized and processed data can be faulty, contain copies, or include mistakes. Data cleaning is the practice of preventing and fixing these mistakes. There are lots of sorts of data cleaning which rely on the sort of information. By way of instance, while cleaning off the fiscal information, specific totals may be compared against trusted printed amounts or defined thresholds. Similarly, qualitative data systems may be used for outlier detection which would be then excluded in diagnosis.

Procedure 5.   Data analysis

Data which is processed, cleaned and organized would be all set for the analysis. Different data analysis methods are readily available to comprehend, interpret, and derive conclusions depending on the requirements. Data visualization might also be utilised to inspect the information in graphic format, to acquire additional insight concerning the messages inside the information.

Statistical data designs like correlation, regression analysis may be employed to spot the connections among the information variables. These models which are descriptive of this information are useful in simplifying investigation and convey results.

The procedure might require further data clean-up or added info collection, and these actions are pragmatic in nature.

Procedure 6.   Communication

The outcome of the data evaluation is to be noted in a format as needed by the consumers to encourage their conclusions and additional actions. The comments from the consumers may lead to further investigation.

The information analysts can select data visualization techniques, like tables and graphs, which assist in conveying the content clearly and economically to the consumers. The study tools offer facility to emphasize the mandatory data with colour filters and codes in tables and graphs.

Data science vs. Data analytics vs. Machine learning: professional chat

Information science, analytics, and machine learning have been growing at an astronomical pace and businesses are currently searching for professionals that will sift through the goldmine of information and let them push fast business decisions economically.

Chapter 5:   Data Science and How It Fits In Machine Learning

Machine learning can definitely be an important part of the Data Science process, as long as we use it properly.

Remember as we go through this process that part of Data Science is working on data analysis. This helps us to take a lot of the data we have collected along the way, and then actually see the insights and the predictions that are inside of it. To make this happen, we need to be able to create our models (that can sort through all of the data), find the hidden patterns, and provide us with our insights.

To define these models, and to make sure that they work the way that we want, we need to have a variety of good algorithms in place, and this is where Machine Learning is going to come into play quite a bit. You will find that with the help of Machine Learning, and the variety of algorithms that are present in Machine Learning, we can create models that can go through any kind of data we have, whether it is big or small, and provide us with the answers that we need here.

Machine learning is a process that we can use to make the system or the machine we are working with think in a manner that humans do. This allows the algorithm to go through and find hidden patterns in the same manner that a human would be able to do, but it can do it much faster and more efficiently than any human could do manually.

Think about how hard this would be to do manually for any human, or even for a group of people who are trying to get through all of that data. It could take them years to get through all of that data and find the insights that they need. And with how fast data are being generated and collected, those predictions and insights would be worthless by the time we got to that point anyway.

Machine learning can make this process so much easier. It allows us to have a way to think through the data and find the hidden patterns and insights that are inside for our needs. With the right Machine Learning algorithm, we can learn how the process works, and all of the steps that are necessary to make this happen for us. With this in mind, it is time to take a closer look at Machine Learning, and all of the parts that we need to know to make this work for our needs.

What is Machine Learning?

The first thing that we need to take a look at here is the basics of Machine Learning. Machine learning is going to be one of the applications of artificial intelligence that can provide a system with the ability to learn, all on its own, without the help of a programmer telling the system what to do. The system can even take this a bit further and can work to improve based on its own experience, and none of this is done with the system being explicitly programmed in the process. The idea of Machine Learning is going to be done with a focus on the development of programs on the computer that can access any data you have, and can then use that presented data to learn something new, and how you would like it to behave.

There are going to be a few different applications that we can look at when it comes to using Machine Learning. As we start to explore more about what Machine Learning can do, you may notice that over the years, it has been able to change and develop into something that programmers are going to enjoy working with more than ever. When you want to make your machine or system do a lot of the work on its own, without you having to step in and program every step, then Machine Learning is the right option for you.

When it comes to the world of technology, we will find that Machine Learning is pretty unique and can add to a level of fun to the coding that we do. There are already a lot of companies, in a variety of industries (which we will talk about in a bit), that will use Machine Learning and are already receiving a ton of benefits from it.

There are a lot of different applications when it comes to using Machine Learning, and it is amazing what all we can do with this kind of artificial intelligence. Some of the best methods that we can follow and focus our time on when it comes to Machine Learning include:

Research on statistics: Machine learning is already making some headway when it comes to the world of IT. You will find that Machine Learning can help you go through a ton of complex data, looking for the large and important patterns that are in the data. Some of the different applications of Machine Learning under this category will include things like spam filtering, credit cards, and search engines.

An analysis of big data: There are a lot of companies who have spent time collecting what is known as Big Data, and now they have to find a way to sort through and learn from that data, in a short amount of time. Companies can use these data to learn more about how money is spent by the customers, and even to help them make important decisions about the future. If we had someone go through and manually do the work, it would take much too long. But with Machine Learning, we can get it all done. Options like the medical field, election campaigns, and even retail stores have started to turn to Machine Learning to gain some of these benefits.

The financial world: Many financial companies have been able to rely on Machine Learning. Stock trading online, for example, will rely on this kind of work, and we will find that Machine Learning can help with fraud detection, loan approvals, and more.

To help us get going with this one, and to understand how we can receive the value that we want out of Machine Learning, we have to make sure that we pair the best algorithms with the right processes and tools. If you are using the wrong kind of algorithm to sort through these data, you are going to get a lot of inaccurate information, and the results will not give you the help that you need. Working with the right algorithm the whole time will make a big difference.

The cool thing that we will see with this one is that there are a lot of Machine Learning algorithms that we can choose from at this point to work on your model. Each of these works in a different manner than the others, but this ensures that you can handle any kind of problem that comes along with your project. With this in mind though, you will notice that some of the different available algorithms include random forests, neural networks, clustering, support vector machines, and more.

As we are working on some of the models that we want to produce, we will also notice that there are a ton of tools and other processes that are available for us to work with. We need to make sure that we pick the right one to ensure that the algorithm and the model that you are working with will perform the way that you would like. The different tools that are available with Machine Learning will include:

Comprehensive management and data quality.

Automated ensemble evaluation of the model to help see where the best performers will show up.

GUIs for helping to build up the models that you want along with the process flows being built up as well.

Easy deployment of this so that you can get results that are reliable and repeatable in a quick manner.

Interactive exploration of the data and even some visualizations that help us to view the information easier.

A platform that is integrated and end to end to help with the automation of some of the data to decision process that you would like to follow.

A tool to compare the different models of Machine Learning to help us identify the best one to use quickly and efficiently

Chapter 6: Data science Algorithms and Models

We took a look at what data analysis is all about, how to work with the Python language and why it is such a good thing for the data analysis, and even some of the basics of Machine Learning and why this should be a part of our process.

We are going to explore some of the best algorithms and models that we can use to complete our data analysis with the help of the Python language. There are so many different algorithms that we can choose from, and all of them are going to be great options to get the work done. With this in mind, let's dive right in and see what some of the best algorithms and models are for completing your business data analysis with Python.

Neural Networks

It is hard to have a discussion about Machine Learning and data analysis without taking some time to talk about neural networks and how these forms of coding are meant to work. Neural networks are a great addition to any Machine Learning model because they can work similarly to the human brain.

With neural networks, each of the layers that you go through will spend a bit of time at that location, seeing if there is any pattern. This is often done with images or videos so it will go through each layer of that image and see whether or not it can find a new pattern. If the network does find one of these patterns, then it is going to instigate the process that it needs to move over to the following layer. This is a process that continues, with the neural network going through many layers until the algorithm has created a good idea of what the image is and can give an accurate prediction.

There are then going to be a few different parts that can show up when we reach this point, and it depends on how the program is set up to work. If the algorithm was able to go through the process above and could sort through all of the different layers, then it is going to make a prediction. If the prediction it provides is right, the neurons in the system will turn out stronger than ever. This is because the program is going to work with artificial intelligence to make the stronger connections and associations that we need to keep this process going. The more times that our neural network can come back with the correct answer, the more efficient this neural network will become in the future when we use it.

When you are working with some of the available conventional coding methods, this process can be really difficult to do. You will find that the neural network system can make this a really easy system to work with.

For the algorithm to work, you would need to provide the system with an image. The neural network would then be able to look over the picture. It would start with the first layer, which would be the outside edges of the object in the image. Then it would go through some other layers that help the neural network understand if any unique characteristics are present in the object. If the program is good at doing the job, it is going to get better at finding some of the smallest details of the object.

There could potentially be a lot of different layers that come with this one, but the more layers and details that the neural network can find, the more accurately it will be able to predict what kind of object is in front of it. If your neural network is accurate in identifying the object, it is going to learn from this lesson. It will remember some of these patterns and characteristics that showed up in the object and will store them for use later.

When working with this algorithm, you are often going to choose one and use it, when you want to go through a large number of pictures and find some of the defining features that are inside of them.

Naïve Bayes

We can also work with an algorithm that is known as the Naïve Bayes algorithm. This is a great algorithm to use any time that you have people who want to see some more of the information that you are working on, and who would like to get more involved in the process, but they are uncertain about how to do this, and may not understand the full extent of what you are doing. It is also helpful if they want to see these results before the algorithm is all the way done.

As you work through some of the other algorithms on this page and see what options are available for handling the data, you will notice that they often take on hundreds of thousands of points of data. This is why it takes some time to train and test the data, and it can be frustrating for those on the outside to find out they need to wait before they can learn anything about the process. Showing information to the people who make the decisions and the key shareholders can be a challenge when you are just getting started with the whole process.

This is where the Naïve Bayes algorithm comes in. It is able to simplify some of the work that you are doing. It will usually not be the final algorithm that you use, but it can often give a good idea to others outside of the process about what you are doing. It can answer questions, puts the work that you are doing in a much easier to understand the form, and can make sure that everyone will be on the same page.

Clustering algorithms

One of the best types of algorithms that you can work with is going to be the clustering algorithm. There are a variety of clustering algorithms out there to focus on, but they are going to help us ensure that the program can learn something on its own, and will be able to handle separating the different data points that we have. These clustering algorithms work best when you can keep things simple. It takes some of the data that you are working with and then makes some clusters that come together. Before we start with the program though, we can choose the number of clusters that we want to fit the information too.

The number of clusters that you go with is going to depend on what kind of information you are working with as well. If you just want to separate your customers by gender, then you can work with just two clusters. If you would like to separate the customers by their age or some other feature, then you may need some more clusters to get this done. You can choose the number of clusters that you would like to work with.

Support Vector Machines

Another option that we need to work with is known as the support vector machine or SVM. When we work with this one, it is important to take all of the items in our data set, and then work on plotting them into one n-dimensional space, rather than having them all over the place. N is going to be the number of features that should show up in this algorithm along with the rest of our information. We then have the option to take the value of all these features and translate them over to the value that is in your coordinates. From here, we determine where the hyperplane is because this will show us the differences that are there between our various classes.

Decision Trees

Decisions trees are also a good option that we can work with when we want to take a few available options, and then compare them to see what the possible outcome of each option is all about. We can even combine a few of these decision trees to make a random forest and get more results and predictions from this.

The decision tree is going to be one of the best ways to compare a lot of options, and then choose the path that is going to be the best for your needs. Sometimes there are a whole host of options that we can choose from, and many times they will all seem like great ideas.

K-Nearest Neighbors

The next algorithm that we can look at is known as the K-Nearest Neighbors algorithm or KNN. When we work with this algorithm, the goal is to search through all of the data that we have for the k most similar example of any instance that we want to work with. Once we can complete this process, then the algorithm can move on to the next step, which is where it will look through all of the information that you have and provide you with a summary. Then the algorithm will take those results and give you some of the predictions you need to make good business decisions.

With this learning algorithm, you will notice that the learning you are working with becomes more competitive. This works to your advantage because there will be a big competition going on between the different elements or the different parts in the models so that you can get the best solution or prediction based on the data you have at hand.

The Markov Algorithm

Another type of unsupervised Machine Learning algorithm that you can work with is the Markov algorithm. This particular algorithm is going to take the data that you decide to input into it, and then it will translate it to help work in another coding language if you choose. The nice thing here is that you can pick out which rules you want to use with this algorithm ahead of time so that the algorithm will work the way that you want. Many programmers in Machine Learning find that this algorithm, and the fact they can set up their own rules ahead of time, is nice because it allows you to take a string of data and ensure that it is as useful as possible as you learn on the job and figure out the parameters of how the data will behave.

Another thing that you may like about this Markov algorithm is that you can work with it in several ways, rather than being stuck with just one method. One option to consider here is that this algorithm works well with things like DNA.

Chapter 7: Python Data Types

The next thing that we need to take a look at is the Python data types. Each value in Python has a type of data.

Since entirety is an object in Python programming, data types are going to be like classes and variables are going to be the instance, which is also known as objects, of these classes. There are a lot of different types of data in Python. Some of the crucial data types that we are able to work with includes:

Python numbers

The first option that we are able to work on Python data includes the Python numbers. These are going to include things like complex numbers, floating-point numbers, and even integers. They are going to be defined as complex, float, and int classes in Python. For example, we are able to work with the type () function to identify which category a value or a variable affiliated with to, and then the insistence () function to audit if an object exists to a distinct class.

When we work with integers can be of any length, it is going to only find limitations in how much memory you have available on your computer. Then there is the floating-point number.

This is going to be accurate up to 15 decimal places, though you can definitely go with a smaller amount as well.

The floating points are going to be separated by a decimal point. 1 is going to be an integer, and 10 will be a floating-point number.

And finally, we have complex numbers. These are going to be the numbers that we will want to write out as x + y, where x is going to be the real point, and then they are going to be the imaginary part.

We need to have these two put together in order to make up the complexity that we need with this kind of number.

Python lists

The next type of data that will show up in the Python language. The Python list is going to be a regulated series of items. It is going to be one of the data types that are used the most in Python, and it is exceedingly responsive.

All of the items that will show up on the list can be similar, but this is not a requirement. You are able to work with a lot of different items on your list, without them being the same type, to make it easier to work with.

Being able to declare a list is going to be a straightforward option that we are able to work with. The items are going to be separated out by commas and then we just need to include them inside some brackets like this: [ ] we can also employ the slicing operator to help us obtain out a piece or a selection of items out of that list.

The index starts at 0 in Python.

And we have to remember while working on these that lists are going to be mutable.

What this means is that the value of the elements that are on your list can be altered in order to meet your own needs overall.

Python Tuple

We can also work with something that is known as a Python Tuple. The Tuple is going to be an ordered series of components that is the duplicate as a list, and it is sometimes hard to see how these are going to be similar and how they are going to be different.

The gigantic diverse that we are going to see with a Tuple and a list is that the tuples are going to be immutable.

Tuples, once you create them, are not modifiable.

Tuples are applied to write-protect data, and we are generally quicker than a list, as they cannot shift actively. It is going to be determined with parentheses () where the items are also going to be separated out by a comma as we see with the lists.

We can then use the slicing operator to help us wring some of the components that we want to use, but we still are not able to change the value while we are working with the code or the program.

Python Strings

Python strings are also important as well. The string is going to be a sequence that will include some Unicode characters.

We can work with either a single quote or a double quote to show off our strings, but we need to make sure that the type of quote that we use at the beginning is the one that we finish it off with, or we will cause some confusion with the compiler.

We can even work with multi-line strings with the help of a triple quite.

Like what we are going to see when we use the tuple or the list that we talked about above, the slicing operator is something that we are able to use with our string as well. And just like with what we see in the tuples, we will find that the string is going to be immutable.

Python Set

Next on the list is going to be the Python set. The set is going to be an option from Python that will include an unordered collection of items that are unique. The set is going to be defined by values that we can separate with a comma in braces. The elements in the batch are not going to be ordered, so we can use them in any manner that we would like.

We have the option to perform this set of operations at the same time as a union or have an intersection on two sets.

The sets that we work with are going to be unique values and they will make sure that we eliminate the duplicates. Since the set is going to be an unordered compilation. Catalogued has no aim.

Therefore, the slicing operator is not going to work for this kind of option.

Python Dictionary

And the final type of Python data that we are going to take a look at is known as the Python dictionary. This is going to be an unordered collection of key-value pairs that we are able to work with. It is generally going to be used when we are working with a very large amount of data. The dictionary can be optimized in such a way that they do a great job of retrieving our data. We have to know the key to retrieve the value ahead of time to make these works.

When we are working with the Python language, a dictionary is going to be decided inside braces, with every component being a combination in the form of key: value. The key and the value can be any type that you would like based on the kind of code that you would like to write. We can also use the key to help us retrieve the respective value that we need. But we are not able to turn this around and work it in that manner at all.

Working with the different types of data is going to be so important for all of the work that you can do in a Python coding, and can help you out when it is time to work with data science.

Take a look at the different types of data that are available with the Python language, and see how great this can be to any of the codes and algorithms that you want to write into your data science project overall.

Chapter 8: Machine Learning Works for Data science

What is Data Science?

Before we are going to take a look at what machine learning, it is time to take a look at the ideas that come with data science. Machine learning is going to be a subset of data science and understanding the whole process of data science is going to be a big thing to consider. We are going to get a better look at data science and why it is so important so that we can get a better look at what machine learning is all about.

It was seen as a main challenge and concern for a lot of industries up until 2010. The main focus here was that the companies wanted to build up a solution and framework to store data.

Now, there were a few frameworks that came out that help to solve the big problem of where to store all of this data. And when that happened, the focus started to shift to how we are able to take a look at this data and process it in the proper way. And this is where data science started to come onto the scene. It is a secret sauce that comes up here.

Why do I need to work with data science?

The first question that we are going to take a look at is the need for data science. In a traditional form, the data that we had to look through was pretty structured and would be small in size. This means that some simple tools were able to go through all of that information. However, the way that we receive the data that comes at us is going to be a bit different now. In fact, we usually end up getting a lot of data that is unstructured or hard to read through.

This is a big issue that you are going to work with when you run a business, but there is a simple solution that is able to help with it. Data science is going to be able to help with this. It is able to take the information that you are given when you look at your customers and then sort it out in a way that you are able to understand and use for making predictions.

It is also possible to use some of the tools that come with data science for predictive analytics. Let's look at the idea of weather forecasting to show us how this works. Data from a lot of different places such as satellites, radars, aircraft, and ships can be collected and then that information is analysed in order to build up some new models.

The Basics of Data Science

We need to take a closer look at data science and what it is all about. You will find that data science is going to be a blend of different machine learning principles, algorithms, and tools that you are able to use, with a goal of discovering the hidden patterns that are going to show up in some of your raw data.

The data analyst is going to spend some time explaining what is going on because they are able to process the history that the data went through. On the other hand, the scientist of data is not only going to do an exploratory analysis in order to figure out what insights are there, but they get the benefit of using some of the more advanced algorithms in machine learning in order to figure out how likely an event is going to happen in the future.

There are a number of tools that you are able to use to make all of this happen. Some of the most prevalent ones that you may want to look through, based on the project that you are focusing your time and attention on will include:

1. Predictive Casual Analytics

If you are looking to use a model that will be able to predict how possible it is that an event is going to happen in the future, then you will want to use this. You will then be able to build up a model that helps you do these analytics based on the past payment history, current debts, and current income of the person to figure out whether they will make their future payments on time or not.

2. Prescriptive Analytics

Another option that you are able to go with here is known as prescriptive analytics. If you are looking to work with a model that is able to make its own decisions, and you can still modify it a bit with some parameters to make it work the way that you want, then this is the one for you.

This is a pretty new field when it comes to data science, but it is able to provide the advice that is needed. It is not only able to take some time predicting a course of action, but it can suggest, from a range of prescribed actions and the associated outcomes, what you need to do next.

3. Using It to Make Some Predictions with Machine Learning

Here is the idea of machine learning that we were talking about before. If you have some data from a finance company, and your goal is to build up a model that is going to show you the future trend of that data, then you want to work with an algorithm that comes from machine learning. This one is going to fall under the category of supervised machine learning, which we will talk about a bit more later.

4. Doing Pattern Discovery with Machine Learning

Another way that you are able to use machine learning to help with data science is going to be with pattern discovery. If you are working on a program and you don't have your own parameters in place for making a prediction, then it is time to find out the hidden patterns that are already in the set of data. This will ensure that you have the right information to make the most accurate of predictions.

This is going to utilize machine learning, and in specific, it is going to work with the unsupervised model of machine learning because it has to learn on its own.

The Lifecycle of Data Science

The next thing that we need to take a look at is the lifecycle of data science. Knowing what this is and how it works is going to make a big difference in the amount of success that you are able to get with this field, and it will help you to get the best results possible out of the process. Some of the steps that come with the data science lifecycle include:

1. Discovery

The first step that we need to explore is going to be the discovery. Before you begin any kind of project in this field, you will need to know the different properties, the requirements, the specifications, and the required budget. Otherwise, it is hard to know where you need to get started. Once you have a bit of this information in place, you will be able to do an assessment of the people, time, data, support, and technology to figure out if the project is something that you will be able to do. If you are short on any of those aspects, then it may be time to evaluate whether or not you would be able to do without them or get them before you start.

2.   Data preparation

When you are done with the steps above, it is time to move on to the second stage. In this one, you are going to need some analysis to see results. You want to have a kind of analytical sandbox in order to perform the right analytics for the whole time that you are working on the project. You will need to explore, take some time to pre-process, and condition the data before you do the modelling.

Once you are done with some of those steps, it is time to go take this a bit further. You will need to do something known as ETLT. This stands for extract, transform, load, and transform. This allows you to get the data that you want into the sandbox so that you can do some of the experiments that you would like to do.

3. Model planning

Once you have been able to clean and prepare any of the data that you would like to use in your models, it is time to actually plan out the models. In this third step, you are going to take some time to determine the proper techniques and models that you want to use in order to draw a good relationship between the variables. You will find, and we will talk about, a lot of different models that you can work with in order to see some separation and understanding of the data, but you need to pick the one that is right for you.

These relationships are important to find and define in the proper manner. These are basically going to set up the base that you need for any algorithm that you want to implement (we will implement these algorithms in the next phase). You will then be able to apply the EDA or the Exploratory Data Analytics using a lot of different visualization tools and even statistical formulas, based on your own needs.

4. Model building

When we get to this phase, you will need to develop some sets of training and testing the data that you have. You first need to take a look at some of the tools that you already have and then decide if they are going to be enough for running the model that you want, or if you need an environment that is more robust. Depending on the kind of algorithm that you want to use, you may need to pick out something that is faster and needs to work with parallel processing instead.

5. Operationalize

Now, we need to move on to the fifth phase. In this one, you have had some time to create a model, use one or more algorithm, and bring in a few different tools. You should have your data organized and ready to use. When you get to this phase, you are going to be able to deliver everything from the technical documents, code documents, briefings, and final reports.

6.   Communicate the results

After you have had the time to present your findings and maybe deploy the model on a small scale, it is time to have some communication about whether or not this was able to achieve its goals. It is important for everyone to come together and really evaluate if they were able to achieve the goals that they set early on in the project.

This means that again you need to do some analysis of what you did throughout and check whether the final results were what you expected. In this last phase, you will need to identify the key findings that showed up, spend some time communicating what happened and how you came to those results with the stakeholders, and then determine whether the results that you saw in the project were a failure or a success based on the goals that you wanted to get in the beginning.

Chapter 9: Use of Python in Machine Learning

Machine learning and associated technologies such as artificial intelligence (AI) are the technologies for the present and future. In a world that is increasingly aggregated towards more personalized gadgets and machines with improved and technical functionalities, tech companies and innovators are on the overdrive, researching, developing, and testing the innovative technologies of the future. These technologies are aimed at revolutionizing the human experience while also cementing the place of machines, especially computers, as the primary drivers of all spheres of human life. While seemingly dedicated to meeting the ever-changing human demand technology and hence, user experience, these companies and individuals are also seeking to develop technologies that can increase their bottom line. These new technologies not only use huge data to execute complex processes that cannot be accomplished manually, but they also come with increased accuracy and efficiency. They can also analyse data patterns to make predictions and come with solutions to problems beforehand. Essentially, machine learning and AI are premised on turning the numerous scientific fictions of the past decades into reality.

However, AI technology comes with the added disadvantage of collecting and analysing a large volume of data to process to execute these complex processes. Additionally, bringing science fiction to life also requires skill sets in programming, creativity, conceptualization, ideation, and analysis. But most importantly, it requires the right programming language that is easier to understand and flexible to work with. The last thing you need as a programmer writing the algorithms for the next game-changer technology that would transform human experiences is being stacked with a programming language that is inflexible and incapable of handling data complexity. This can easily lead to errors in the coding of the machine's program or applications. A code error can lead to embarrassing situations for developers, as exemplified in the 2016 case involving Microsoft's chatbot, which malfunctioned and resorted to communicating misogynistic messages to the millennials instead of the intended happy and positive themed messages. Amazon, the world's leading online retailer, also suffered reputational damage in 2014 when its AI machine, designed for talent recruitment, turned in a discriminative tool that singled out female applicants. These are just a few cases involving well-established tech giants whose Machine Learning and AI algorithms were erratic due to programming issues.

Python and AI and ML

Training a computer to possess the human-like ability of learning and making predictions without continuous specific process-based programming can be a daunting task without the right programming language. By eliminating the need for explicit programming, a program developer would then need to feed the computer the right training data that the computer will use as a point of reference, more like a library to learn from. This is one of the primary points of departures between traditional and non-traditional programming projects such as IA or machine learning. Using the training data, a programmer will be able to develop a software using numerous lines of codes to create the desired algorithms for the machine. However, such a complex project requires a mastery of statistics and mathematical optimization to achieve the best result: an algorithm free of coding errors, which can lead to machine malfunctioning. Additionally, a programmer should also understand the concept of probability to ensure that the developed algorithms are capable of making predictions, which one of the primary functional capabilities of machines equipped with AI capabilities.

To facilitate the execution of such complex programming tasks, Python, a programming language conceived by the software engineering guru Guido van Rossum, is equipped with various libraries or modules. These modules come in handy for programmers when coding as they have inbuilt code pieces that are already written. Programmers can use these pre-written codes as the backbone of the algorithms they are aiming to write for a specific project. With a pre-existing code, a programmer has the jumpstart to develop even complex algorithms that artificial intelligence-based technologies require. This is because the codes that come with the programming language modules have level items that support basic functionalities. They also act as launch pads for the next set of coding actions, thereby eliminating the need for starting any programming project afresh.

Python's extensive library ecosystem includes Scikit-learn, Seaborn, NumPy, and Pandas. Others include Keras and SciPy. These sets of libraries are specialized for different tasks during the development of algorithms for AI and machine learning. For example, Seaborn module is primarily used for coding tasks involving visualization of training data to be used in machine learning. This includes the exploration of data with the view of plotting statistical patterns. It is from these patterns that machines use their AI to project scenarios.

On the other hand, Pandas is readily the most popular set of libraries among programmers using Python language because of its functional versatility. The module is suitable for all forms of coding-related data analysis. As an object-oriented language, Python relies heavily on the analysis and interpretation of these data during coding to develop algorithms that the machine can learn from and use the knowledge to make predictions. This is why SciPy and NumPy are the most important Python libraries. The bulk of Python programming-related projects use these two libraries. NumPy lacks the general-purpose nature of Pandas, even though it is also used for analysing coding data. However, it is most suitable for analysing high-performance data.

Scikit-learn library is the most flexible of all these modules and plays an important role in the overall simplicity, flexibility, and versatility of Python as a programming language. It can be easily integrated with other modules such as NumPy and SciPy, to achieve greater coding success. Programmers using Scikit-learn library will find it easy to implement tasks during coding, as this will take only a few lines to accomplish. Such functional simplicity in task implementation is because Scikit-learn is compatible with unsupervised and supervised algorithms, a variety of algorithms that machine learning and AI rely on to achieve functional autonomy. Therefore, coding that involves probability testing, mathematical optimization, and statistics such as regressions, decision trees, and k-means are easily executed using the Scikit-learn library set.

Basics of Using Python Modules in Machine Learning Projects

The first step towards developing algorithms for your machine learning project using Python programming language is problem identification. Programming for machine learning is a targeted undertaking aimed at tackling a specific problem. Therefore, when fully defined, a problem will help the programmer in developing the parameters of the algorithm and the data set to be collected. Defining a problem directs the whole coding process. It will determine what kind of predictions that machine will be able to make as well as identifying its functional integrity. That is, identifying the integrity of the algorithm and the program used by the machine.

Secondly, determine whether your version comes with or without pre-bundled modules. Python's anaconda and miniconda packages usually come with the fundamental module: SciPy Libraries. Upon installation, SciPy libraries come with preinstalled modules such as NumPy, Scikit-learn, Pandas, and SciPy, among others. In case the Python package does not come with SciPy libraries, download the library and install it. For pre-bundled packages, use the cmd command and type the specific name of the module to install. Always make sure that your versions of the bundles are updated. Using the latest version of modules will allow the programmer to access new and better features that improve the integrity of their software or applications.

After installing and updating Python and the modules, you must import all the relevant objects and modules that will be required during the coding process. The type of libraries imported is dependent on the dataset and the functional capability that the algorithms are projected to achieve. This should be followed by loading the dataset to be used for machine learning from the relevant source suing the Pandas modules. The loaded training data should be prepared appropriately to meet the project needs. It should be large enough to improve the accuracy of the predictions of the machine. Adding randomness links to your training dataset will improve the machine's ability to make predictions. In case you are using a hosted version of the dataset due to unreliability issues, it is always advisable to include a link to it. This will reduce cases of coding errors as a result of using redundant datasets.

A dataset summary will give the programmer insights on his or her dataset dimensions, including classes and attributes such as some data columns. Additionally, it shows a brief overview of the dataset. A programmer also has the chance to discern the various statistical attributes associated with the data they are using for coding. After summarizing, it is advisable to visualize the dataset using either univariate or multivariate plots. Plotting allows a programmer to have a greater understating of the relationships between the various variables within the dataset to be used in developing algorithms for the machine. Data visualization is done using Pandas libraries, which has different options for visualization, including scatterplots and distribution graphs. Testing the dataset using models and a validation dataset before developing the final algorithms for machine learning is very important. The validation dataset will act as your point of reference whenever you are using the algorithms to predict unseen datasets. Moreover, it also acts as a starting for any further changes and improvements you will need to make on the algorithms; it eliminates the need to start all over again in case of a coding error.

Benefits of Using Python in M.L. and A.I.

One of the reasons behind Python's growing popularity as a programming language of choice for many programmers is its relatively large library ecosystem. Python's library ecosystem is comprised of numerous modules and extensions that support the implementation of a wide range of coding tasks, including data analysis and visualization, among others. From Pandas to SciPy, NumPy and Keras, Python has a wide range of libraries that gives it the versatility needed to code even for complex algorithms.

It also boasts of simple syntaxes and semantics that are easy to follow and use. They have a math-like characters which make them easier to familiarize with when coding. This makes coding with Python easier and less technical. Mastering basic coding using Python does not require technical know-how. This makes coding preferable among basic users as opposed to other mainstream programming languages such as Java and C. It is also a general-purpose language that makes it easy to use to develop a wide range of algorithms for machine learning.

Chapter 10:

Functions in Python

Here are the functions that are a piece of code that can be executed repeatedly with different variables to generate a different outcome.

Function Utilities in Programming

Functions are a fundamental concept in any programming language. They are also known as procedures or routines in other programming languages. Functions are very handy when you need to run the same code with different variable values. For instance, you want to compute the factorial of different numbers. Instead of coding the same code for each number, you would define a function that takes as input the number of interests, computes its factorial, and returns the result. This way you just have to call the same function for each number inside a loop for instance.

In this context, functions serve for two main purposes. The first is to make the code reusable. They provide a way to package your code such that it is used more than once or in multiple places in the same or different program.

With functions, the code can be wrapped and generalized to be used several times after. The second purpose of functions is to decompose a program into several pieces where each piece is assigned a role. This is very useful when coding a large program or a framework that replicates the functioning of a complex system. Functions allow us to break down the system into pieces where each piece is coded by a function. Each function would serve to perform a task in a large system. This way of coding makes it easy to implement complex systems than just implementing a whole system in one chunk of code. You can think of functions as a procedure that allows replicating how to do something. Coding functions does not imply different syntax.

Function Concept, Declaration and Calling in Python

We have been using and calling functions that are built-in Python. For example, to compute the length of an object, we call the function len. Every new function you define in Python works exactly the same as the built-in functions of Python. Functions are called through statements or expressions and can take input arguments and return a result. In Python, functions act differently compared to complied programming languages (e.g. C or C++).

'def ', a new statement, defines the Python functions. This is also an executable code. When you develop a new function, it is not recognized by the Python until it hits a 'def ' statement and runs through it. Sometimes, the 'def ' statement is inserted in if test or a loop or maybe inside other 'def ' statement. In a real application, the 'def ' statements are defined within modules. When the module is imported in the Python environment workspace, the functions are generated automatically. The 'def ' statement makes a new object (i.e. a function) and assigns a name to it. A function object is created and given a name every time a 'def ' statement is found by Python. This name is the reference of the function which can be saved in a list or given another name. Functions can send back an object result after they are called. When Python goes through a statement that calls a function, it runs through the function code until it finishes. Then it resumes to the following statements. If a function returns a value, it communicates it back to the control flow as a return statement. This result is then the outcome of calling this function. Functions can take optionally input arguments that passed as a reference.

Unlike other programming languages such as C or C++, references (i.e. variables) are shared across the function and Python called. This means that a variable that is modified within a function is also modified automatically within the entire code. In other words, if you define a variable name outside a function. Then, later in the code, you call a function that shares the same variable name (i.e. reference) that changes its values. When the function is finished running and the control is given back to the controller, the variable has the same value that was assigned inside the function and not the value that was assigned before the function call.

Variables that are assigned inside a function are, by default, local variables. They are defined only inside the function. Once the function finishes running, these variables don't exist anymore. Like any other object data, the function does not need any declaration of any kind prior to use. Inputs arguments, as well as output arguments, can be of any type of data object. Hence, the functions can be called with different data types.

To create a new function, we use the 'def ' statement with the following syntax:

def < function name> (argument 1, ..., argument n):

statements or tasks to perform

Like any compound statement in Python, indentation is very imported. All statements that constitute the function body should be intended unless it is one single statement that can appear after the header (i.e. after the colon). The function body is executed every time the function is called. After 'def ' is the name of the function which attributed to reference to the function object, followed by the arguments. The name of arguments is attributed to the data object that is passed to the function when called. If no argument is to be passed to the function, then the syntax is as follows:

def < function name> ():

statements or tasks to perform

Usually, a function returns an output argument or statement. In this case, the syntax of the function includes a return statement as follow:

def < function name> (argument 1, ..., argument n):

statements or tasks to perform

return < output value>

In Python, the 'def ' can appear anywhere in the code, even inside other statement. For example, we can define a function according to a test like follows:

If < condition >:

```
def my_function():
```

```
statement 1
```

```
else:
```

```
def my_function(argument):
```

```
statement 2
```

In the syntax example given above, the function my_function is defined with or without input argument depending on whether the condition is satisfied or not. The 'def ' statement works as any Python assignment statement and the function is not defined until the code goes through the 'def ' statement. The function name can also be changed anytime by assigning it to another name. For instance, we can do:

```
Name2= my_function
```

To call a function we just type in the name of the function with arguments if it takes any.

```
function_name (argument 1, argument 2, ..., argument 3)
```

Or function_name ()

W are going to present explicitly how functions use arguments and return values with some examples.

Function Expressions, Arguments, and Returned outputs

Arguments of a function, also called parameters, are passed between parenthesis. When the function is called, Python uses these arguments to reference the date object passed as input. There is no requirement to declare the type of the data object that the function is expecting as input. Usually, functions are defined within modules and run outside of the interactive session. For the sake of simplicity and the fact we are using simple basic examples, the interactive prompt would be sufficient to run the examples

The following code is an example of a function that takes as an argument a number, computes and displays a factorial of a number.

>>> def Xfactorial (X):

... P = 1

... for i in range (1, X + 1):

*... P *= i*

... print ('Factorial of ', X, 'is:', P)

Now, to call this function, we simply type the name of the function with the number for which we want to compute the factorial. For example:

>>> Xfactorial (3)

Factorial of 3 is: 6

If we want to save the output of this function in a later use in the code, we use the return statement when defining the function as follows:

>>> def Xfactorial (X):

... P = 1

... for i in range (1, X + 1):

*... P *= i*

... return P

Then when calling the function, we assign the function to a variable as follows:

>>> A = Xfactorial (3)

>>> print ('Factorial 3 is:', A)

Factorial 3 is: 6

Now, let's consider a simple function that returns the value of X times Y with X and Y two input arguments.

>>> def Prod (A, B):

*... return A * B*

Now, let's call this function with input arguments of different types.

```
>>> A = Prod (2, 3)

>>> print ('This is an example of calling the Prod function with two integers:', A)

This is an example of calling the Prod function with two integers: 6

>>> A = Prod (1.5, 3)

>>> print ('This is an example of calling the Prod function with a float and integer:', A)

This is an example of calling the Prod function with a float and integer: 4.5

>>> A = Prod ('name', 3)

>>> print ('This is an example of calling the Prod function with a string and integer\n:', A)

This is an example of calling the Prod function with a string and integer:

namenamename

>>> A = Prod ('name', 'name')

Traceback (most recent call last):

 File "<stdin>", line 1, in <module>
```

File "<stdin>", line 2, in Prod

TypeError: can't multiply sequence by non-int of type 'str'

In the examples above, we called the function and passed two integers, a float and integer, and a string and an integer. In the first case, it returned an integer. In the second, it returned a float, and in the third, it returned a string. In the final example, we passed two strings input arguments and Python raised an error because multiplication between strings does not exit. Overall, there is no declaration or restriction on the data type that can be passed to a function as long as the operations in the function body are defined.

Overall, Python functions allow defining code scripts that are reusable as many times as it is needed. There are no restrictions on the data object type passed as arguments. The code becomes general and used in any context as long as the operations inside the function are defined. Moreover, you can define your own operations inside these functions or include exception statements that can handle issues in this case. By coding a script within a function, it makes it easy to make a modification if needed and to be made in one single place. You can also insert a function code within a module file.

This way, the function can be imported by importing the module and used within any program or shared with other programs for wide broad use. In fact, this is exactly how packages are developed and used in Python.

and Tricks for an Expert Phyton Programming

Now that we have taken some time to learn more about Python and all of the aspects that come with data science and machine learning, it is time to make sure that we can get the Python up and running. It can be hard as a beginner to learn how to make this kind of programming work for your needs. Some of the different things that you can try out to help you get the most out of some of your coding in Python, and to ensure that you are able to handle all of the different parts of your coding language will include:

Do Only a Few Lines of Code at a Time

One of the worst things that you are able to do when it comes to coding in the Python language or really any language for that matter, is that you will sit down at the computer, and then spend all day writing code. You have a great idea that you want to get out and experiment with, and you just let your fingers type in code for hours on end, without tiring at all. During this time, you don't take a break, but you also don't check any of the code that you have created to see whether it is working or not.

Now that you are done with doing all of that coding, it is time to go through and test it out to see whether this works or not. And surprise, you have a bunch of error messages that pop up (because you are just learning how to code), and you are not sure how to handle this issue. It is going to take you twice as long to read back through the code and to figure out where those errors are, and how you are able to fix them for your needs.

The good news here is that there is a simple solution that you are able to work with that will ensure that you never get stuck in this situation again. And that is simply the idea that you need to go through and, rather than sitting down and writing pages of code all at once, you write small bits of code, and then run it to see whether it works or not.

If you work with this language in the right way, you will find that taking small bits of code will help you, whether there is an error or not. If an error does show up in some of the coding that you write, you will know exactly where that error occurred.

When that time frame is up, you can try to have the compiler run it all and see what happens. If you have an error, think about how much easier it is to find that error and correct it when you only have maybe a page of code or less to deal with. Keep yourself on this kind of schedule. It may seem like you are slowing down and not getting much done, but in the long run, it is going to be one of the best things that you can do.

Ask for Help

There are many people online who can provide advice, and sometimes you may even know some individuals who are good at programming and who would be willing to walk you through the steps and ensure you get things done.

Asking for help when you get started with Python, or with any other coding language, is going to be hard. One of the best ways that you are able to learn how to code, especially with Python, is to ask for help from someone else.

Now, there are a few things that you are able to do in order to get started with asking for help. You want to make sure that the other person knows what is going on in the code, what your goals were on writing that code, and what you have tried to help with fixing that code as well. This will ensure that you are able to get the code done and that the other person is not wasting their time doing things that you have already done. With this in mind, some of the steps that you should take when you ask for help from another person on your own codes include:

Tell the other person what your plans are with that code. This is going to help them to get some background and will allow them to figure out where some of the potential problems are going to lie in the process as well.

Tell them where you have gotten stuck on the code. Once the other person who is helping you understands more about the code that you are trying to create and run, it is time for you to go through and let them know the specific spot in the code where you have gotten stuck.

Share some of the error messages that have come up with that part of the code. You need to share any information that was in the error message as well.

Let them know what steps you have taken in order to handle the code and to try and fix the problem.. Remember that the other person is trying to provide you with some of the help and the assistance that you are looking for, so being open and honest with what has worked and what has not worked, and what you have tired, can speed up the process and help you to get back to some of your coding as well.

Comment out the Code

Sometimes, when there is a problem with your code and you are not sure how to handle it, or where the error is, you can find that commenting out the code is going to be the best way to figure out what is wrong and what is working the best. If you comment out the piece of code and then the rest works fine, then this is a hint that the error is going to be located in that area.

What we need to do to make this part work is to comment out the parts of code, starting at the area where you know for sure that the code was working last. So, maybe you checked the code twenty minutes ago and it worked, but then you spent some time writing code and it doesn't work all of a sudden. You would start by commenting out all of the code that you wrote at that time and work backward from there.

Before we dive into this, remember that commenting out in Python is pretty easy. You just need to use the # symbol in order to get started. This will tell the compiler to just skip over that part of the code. So the Python compiler will assume that there is nothing in that part of the code and that those lines don't exist.

Once all of the code that you are worried about is commented out, it is time for us to go through and uncomment one part at a time. Going from the top and working our way down, take one part and uncomment it before running the code again. So, if you created a class, you can uncomment the class and see if the code works well up to that point. If you wrote out a conditional statement or a loop, you would go through and uncomment that out and see whether the code will start to work.

Once you have been able to figure out where the error is located, you will be able to work on fixing it. It is often best to still work through the uncommenting process until all of the code is up and running again though.

Consider Learning About Some Error Messages

Learning about some of the most common errors that programmers make can help out. This will ensure that you understand some of the error messages that show up as you run and test your code. You don't have to memorize all of them, as there are quite a few that you need to be worried about. But learning the ones that you are most likely to encounter, at least a few of them along the way, can make a big difference in how quickly you can solve the problem and move on to other parts of coding.

If you don't know about the error and it is not on your list of ones to keep in mind, this doesn't mean that you are lost. There are a few methods that you can use to take care of these errors as well. First, actually read through and see what the error message says.

Don't assume that just because an error message has shown up on the screen that all hope is lost and you will never be able to figure out what is wrong. You may be surprised at how much you will be able to understand when it comes to these error messages, and just reading through it really quick can help you to figure out what is wrong with the code, and what you need to go through and fix. If nothing else, it is worth a shot and could save you a lot of time in the process.

If you are still struggling to figure out what the error is all about, or it comes back as a weird list of numbers and letters that make no sense to you, then it is time to head to Google or another search engine and snoop around.

Since it is likely that someone else has gone through the same kind of issue with their project, it will be easy for you to find the solution. You can then use that to help you fix the issue and get your own code up and running. If you can't read what the error message says or figure out what is wrong on your own, looking through the community of other great Python programmers is one of the best ways to get yourself going again, and a quick search engine query can get this done.

The good news with this one is that if you took breaks and you only did a few lines of code before testing it out, you should be able to find the error message fairly quickly, and it is going to be easier for you to go into the code and make the changes. Sometimes, just knowing that there is an error in a small block of code can get you back there and figuring out what it means on your own.

Working with the Python language can be a great experience for many programmers. It ensures that we are able to handle some of the different parts of our data analysis and machine learning, and will make it easier to get some of the coding done that we want.

Chapter 12: Performed Python Programming Exercises

MySql Connector in Python

Follow the steps:

1. Start PC and type cmd in search, click upon it to bring the command prompt

2. Locate where pip is within Python sub directory it can be in C:\Program Files\XYZ\Python37\Scripts

3. Go to the sub directory by giving DOS command Dos Prompt>cd\program files\xyz\python37\scripts

4. Then type the following to install mysql connector python -m pip install mysql-connector

```
ython37\Scripts>python -m pip install mysql connector
```

How to fix the problems

First upgrade pip to latest version if required, you can do this every week

```
m Files\Python37\Scripts>python -m pip install --upgrade pip
g pip
ding https://files.pythonhosted.org/packages/54/0c/d01aa759fdc501a58f43
495f15b88da142ce14b5845662c13f3/pip-20.0.2-py2.py3-none-any.whl (1.4MB)
                                    | 1.0MB 262kB/s eta 0:00:02
```

For applicable for all users give the command

```
Files\Python37\Scripts>python -m pip install --upgrade pip --user
pip
hed https://files.pythonhosted.org/packages/54/0c/d01aa759fdc501a58f4
95f15b88da142ce14b5845662c13f3/pip-20.0.2-py2.py3-none-any.whl
collected packages: pip
y installed pip-20.0.2
```

You should get this message

Finally run the command to install mysql connector as shown

```
rogram Files\Python37\Scripts>python -m pip install mysql-connector --user
ecting mysql-connector
wnloading mysql-connector-2.2.9.tar.gz (11.9 MB)
    |                    | 2.8 MB 544 kB/s eta 0:00:17
```

If successful you should get this, pretty simple isn't?

```
Installing collected packages: mysql-connector
    Running setup.py install for mysql-connector ... done
Successfully installed mysql-connector-2.2.9
```

Open mysql prompt and see the list of databases

```
mysql> show databases;
+--------------------+
| Database           |
+--------------------+
| information_schema |
| mysql              |
| test               |
+--------------------+
3 rows in set (0.64 sec)
```

Check the user and localhost also using this command

```
mysql> select USER();
+----------------+
| USER()         |
+----------------+
| root@localhost |
+----------------+
1 row in set (1.13 sec)
mysql>
```

Now let's see it from Python! Open a new file in Python (.py) and type as it is

ipmort mysql.connector

spcdatabase = mysql.connector (#just giving a name to my connection

host="localhost', #as you can see in select USER() command

user ="root",

password=" ")

Spccur=spcdatabase.cusor() #cursor() method is called by the connection again in spccur

Spccure.execute("show databases")

for i in spccur:

   print(i)

For your convinence I'm attaching a .txt also of the code

```
import mysql.connector
spcdatabase = mysql.connector.connect ( # just giving a name to my connection host="localhost", # as you can see in select USER() command user="root",
password=" "
spccur=spcdatabase.cursor() # cursor() method is called by the connection again stored in spccur spccur.execute("show databases")
for i in spccur: print(i)
```

When you run you see

('information_schema',)

('mysql',)

('test',)

>>>

Cross check it's same databases as you have seen.

Let's try to create a database name virus and a table under the database as coronavirus. We will add the fields province, country and transmission_type in the table initially and add few records. After that we will alter the table and add another field which is primary key name is record_id type integer. For simplicity we have taken all other fields as varchar.

The following script will create a database and also will display the list of databases present.

('information_schema',)

('mysql',)

('test',)

('virus',)

It will display the output as shown below, notice that database virus is created. [You can actually at this point check it in mysql also] Cross check in MySql and its there

```
mysql> show databases;
+--------------------+
| Database           |
+--------------------+
| information_schema |
| mysql              |
| test               |
| virus              |
+--------------------+
4 rows in set (0.00 sec)
```

Remember to run it only once otherwise it will display an error as the database is already created.

Mysql.connector.errors.DtabaseError:1007 (HY000):Can't create database 'virus'; database exist

Once the database is there, we can have the table coronavirus

The following code will create a table corona under database virus

Import mysql.connector

Spcdatabase=mysql.connector.connect(

Host="localhost"

user = "root"

password = "   "

database = "virus"

)

Spccur=spcdatabase.cursor()

Spccur.execute("create table corona(province varchar(30), country varchar(30), transmission_typevarchar(30))')

Spccur.execute("show tables") #our database is set to virus

For I in spccur:

print(i)

The output is shown below:

('corona',)

We can cross check in MySql the see the table created

```
mysql> use virus;
Database changed
mysql> show tables;
+------------------+
| Tables_in_virus |
+------------------+
| corona           |
+------------------+
1 row in set (0.00 sec)
```

For your convinence I'm attaching a .txt also of the Python code
import   mysql.connector

```python
spcdatabase=mysql.connector.connect(
host="localhost",
user="root",
password="                                    ",
database="virus"

   spccur=spcdatabase.cursor()
spccur.execute("create table corona(province varchar(30), country
varchar(30), transmission_type varchar(30))")

   spccur.execute("show tables") # our database is set to virus
for i in spccur:

      print(i)
```

Suppose we need to display the table structure we change the code a
little

```python
   import mysql.connector

   Spcdatabase=mysql.connector.connect(

   Host="localhost"

   user = "root"

   password = "   "

   database = "virus"

   )
```

spccur=spcdatabase.cursor()

spccur.execute("show columns from corona")

for i in spccur:

print(i)

The output is shown as below

In case you want to see the same in MySql

```
mysql> show columns from corona;
+------------------+-------------+------+-----+---------+-------+
| Field            | Type        | Null | Key | Default | Extra |
+------------------+-------------+------+-----+---------+-------+
| province         | varchar(30) | YES  |     | NULL    |       |
| country          | varchar(30) | YES  |     | NULL    |       |
| transmission_type| varchar(30) | YES  |     | NULL    |       |
+------------------+-------------+------+-----+---------+-------+
3 rows in set (0.00 sec)
```

If we now require to alter the table and add a primary key, we modify

the code as:

import mysql.connector

Spcdatabase=mysql.connector.connect(

Host="localhost"

user = "root"

```
        password = "    "

        database = "virus"

    )



    spccur=spcdatabase.cursor()

    spccur.execute("alter table from corona add column record_id int
primary key first")



    spccur.execute(show columns from corona"

    for i in spccur:

        print(i)
```

The output is as below, a primary key is added as shown:

```
('record_id', 'int(11)', 'NO', 'PRI', None, '')
('province', 'varchar(30)', 'YES', '', None, '')
('country', 'varchar(30)', 'YES', '', None, '')
('transmission_type', 'varchar(30)', 'YES', '', None, '')
```

Let's add some records now:

```
import mysql.connector

spcdatabase=mysql.connector.connect(
    host="localhost",
    user="root",
    password="   ",
    database="virus"
    )

spccur=spcdatabase.cursor()
spccur.execute("insert into corona values(1,'Wuhan','China','Local')")

spccur.execute("select *from corona")
for i in spccur:
    print(i)
```

Output is

(1, 'Wuhan', 'China', 'Local')

But if we check in MySql we don't find any records

```
mysql> select * from corona;
Empty set (0.00 sec)
```

because to write in the table we must add the statement

spcdatabase.commit() so the code must be modified as

```
import mysql.connector

spcdatabase=mysql.connector.connect(
    host="localhost",
    user="root",
    password="   ",
    database="virus"
    )

spccur=spcdatabase.cursor()
spccur.execute("insert into corona values(1,'Wuhan','China','Local')")
spcdatabase.commit()
spccur.execute("select *from corona")
for i in spccur:
    print(i)
```

```
mysql> select * from corona;
+-----------+----------+---------+-------------------+
| record_id | province | country | transmission_type |
+-----------+----------+---------+-------------------+
|         1 | Wuhan    | China   | Local             |
+-----------+----------+---------+-------------------+
1 row in set (0.00 sec)
```

Let's add few more records and display all records

```python
import mysql.connector

spcdatabase=mysql.connector.connect(
    host="localhost",
    user="root",
    password="    ",
    database="virus"
    )

spccur=spcdatabase.cursor()
spccur.execute("select *from corona")
for i in spccur:
    print(i)
```

Output is as below

(1, 'Wuhan', 'China', 'Local')

(2, 'Huanan', 'China', 'Local')

(3, 'Patong','Thailand','Imported')

(4, 'WashingtonDC', 'USA', 'Imported')

(5, 'Milan', 'Italy', 'Imported')

(7, 'Mitterteich', 'Germany', 'Imported')

(8, 'Hurghada', 'Iran', 'Imported')

Let's do some query what about displaying only records where local transmission has happened:

Import mysql.connector

Spcdatabase=mysql.connectorr.connect(

Host="localhost"

User="root"

Password=" "

Database"virus"

)

Output is

(1, 'Wuhan', 'China', 'Local')

(2, 'Huanan', 'China', 'Local')

We can in fact do complex queries also

Import mysql.connector

```
Spcdatabase=mysql.connector.connect(

Host="localhost"

User="root"

Password= "    "

D

database = "virus"

)

Spccur=spcdatabase.cursor()

Spccur.execute("select *from corona where province like 'M%' or
country like 'T%'")

for I in spccur:

print(i)


Output

(3, 'Patong','Thailand','Imported')

(4, 'WashingtonDC', 'USA', 'Imported')

(5, 'Milan', 'Italy', 'Imported')

(7, 'Mitterteich', 'Germany', 'Imported')
```

Conclusion

Python is a programming language that has gained popularity in the last few years due to its simple and flexible syntax and the highly efficient functions and tools that come with it. As an object-oriented scripting language, Python can be used for coding of both web pages and applications algorithms or codes. It is applied in many fields and used by web developers and scientists around the world. It is easy to understand and therefore does require a lot of technical knowhow by the users. This is unlike other programming languages such as Java which are a little technical. Python tools and functions include: Working with Inheritance in Python, Working with Iterators in Python, Python Generators, Itertools in the Python language, and Closure in Python.

These tools and functions make Python language suitable for complex and simple coding projects since it is clean and the length of the codes is short compared to others. Moreover, it is exciting to work in Python because it enables you to focus on the challenge instead of the syntax.

Itertools in the Python language are modules that implement iterator building blocks. The work of itertools is to produce complex iterators.

Working with iterators in Python require skills and focus. Python generators are used to create iterators. There are numerous overheads that exists in creating iterators in Python. Python generators handle all the overhead. In simple terms, a generator is used to return objects (iterators) that can be iterated. It is easy to create a generator in Python once you understand how it works. The generator function is one of the best and notable features of the Python programming language. You can find several articles on the Internet that describe the benefits of using generators in Python, including speed, memory efficiency, and scalability.

However, there is limited information on how the generator function works. What many writers do not tell you is that generators work well in Python. The best part of the generator feature is that it can be paused and resumed later, unlike other functions. When the function is paused, the local state is kept intact until the user is ready to resume functions again. Generators are written functions using the yield statement instead of the return statement. It is an effective tool for implementing iterators.

One of the distinctive properties of generators is the ability to connect with other generators and generator expressions to form a long chain of data processing pipeline. Pipelining of data is a critical organizational process that allows for processing of large amounts of data for strategic decision making. When connected, a chain of generators works efficiently to process complex sequences into a single match, each at a time, with the output from the previous generator becoming the input for the next generator.

Moreover, it is convenient and easy to implement because it facilitates the evaluation of elements, unlike regular functions. The generator is preferred because it takes less memory. List comprehensions form part of functional programming in Python language. It allows users to create lists using a for-loop. Generator expressions are limited and one can only do so much with them.

However, this does not mean that you cannot do interesting things with generator expressions Closures are preferred by many because they avoid the use of global variables. In cases where there are few methods in class, opt for closures. You can make a Python closure and a nested loop to make functions and get numerous multiplication functions by employing closures. Moreover, you can use closures to make multiply with 5 () easily. Using closures in Python makes learning fun and exciting. Closures are mostly used when the person. Several documentations about closures and programming focus on front-end development. A function is the most popular unit of scope, and every function declared results in an individual scope